GREENHOUSEMUSICAK.COM

Composing

Your Dream Job

Turning your passion for music into a career

Delana Green

Everything you need to know to get your new business up and running!

Table of Contents

Why this is the book you should read?

A beginning entrepreneur who dreams of starting their own private music studio would benefit greatly from reading "Composing your dream job." This book provides a comprehensive guide to building a successful music studio from scratch, covering everything from designing a studio space to creating lesson plans and managing instructors.

The book offers practical advice and valuable insights on starting a business in the music industry, a niche that can be both challenging and rewarding. It also provides tips on how to market and promote a music studio, establish partnerships with other businesses and organizations, and build a strong online presence.

Whether you are a musician looking to turn your passion into a career, or an aspiring entrepreneur who wants to make a difference in the world of music education, "Composing your dream job" offers a step-by-step guide to building a successful private music studio.

With this book, you can gain the knowledge and confidence needed to turn your dreams into a reality and build a thriving business doing what you love.

The Author

HELLO THERE! I'M DELANA

I'm Delana and I sip my morning latte in the grand state of Alaska.

I have been a business owner for 11 years. I've got an awesome husband and three little girls. I'm one of those people that loves to wear many hats. I've been a national speaker, playwright, T.V. personality, podcast host, author, and more.

My full-time business is my main passion. I am a Music Educator with online music courses and an in-person studio: Greenhouse Music.

I love building communities in the business world and helping out early entrepreneurs thrive with their businesses.

Stay tuned for more books in the pipeline.

GREENHOUSEMUSICAK.COM

Chapter One

Hitting the Right Note -

Introduction to Owning a Private Music Studio

From Humming to Hustling:

So, Have you ever dreamed of turning your love of music into a full-time career? Well, let me tell you, owning a private music studio is the ultimate way to rock your mom/dad-preneur game.

Why do you ask? For starters, you get to be your own boss! No more taking orders from the big guys in suits who don't understand the magic of a perfect chord progression. Plus, you get to create a safe and welcoming space where you can share your love of music with budding musicians of all ages. Let's not forget the perksof working from home.

Now, a few things I want to mention before we truly dive into everything. Here are some keywords you might see me use. and the definitions.

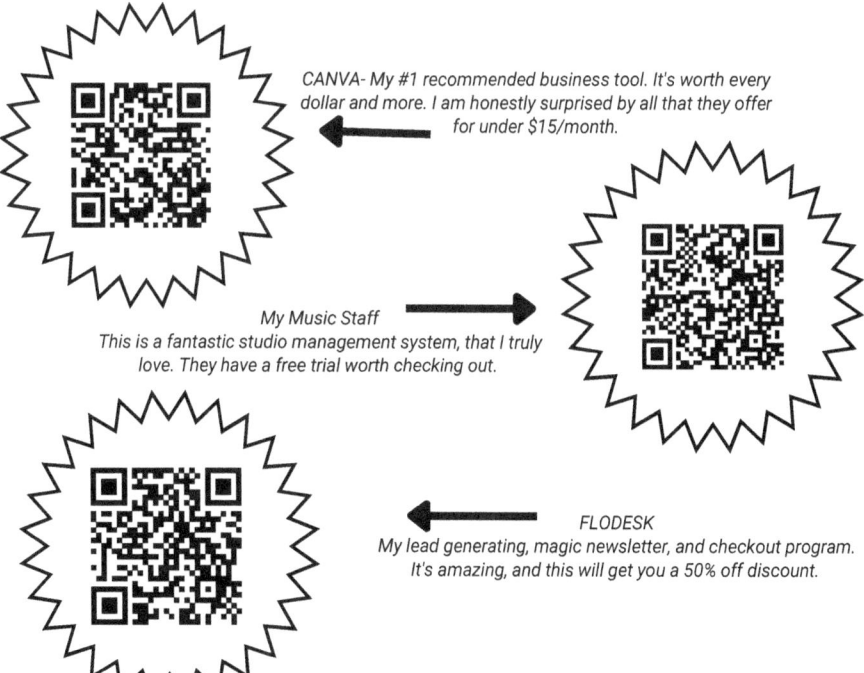

CANVA- My #1 recommended business tool. It's worth every dollar and more. I am honestly surprised by all that they offer for under $15/month.

My Music Staff
This is a fantastic studio management system, that I truly love. They have a free trial worth checking out.

FLODESK
My lead generating, magic newsletter, and checkout program. It's amazing, and this will get you a 50% off discount.

Say goodbye to commuting in traffic and hello to working in your cozy pajamas while sipping on a cup of coffee. You can even set your own hours, so you never have to miss a school play or a soccer game again. But before you start strumming your guitar and singing "I Will Survive" at the top of your lungs, it's important to have a solid plan. In the following chapters, we'll cover everything from creating a business plan to building your studio space and hiring instructors.

So get ready to rock and roll, my fellow entrepreneurs! We're about to embark on a journey that will take us from humming to hustling. Let's compose our dream jobs, one note at a time!

Why Owning a Private Music Studio is the Best Gig.

The best?! Really? Delana, are you positive? 100%! Especially if you are a parent. Don't worry, there are so many perfect tidbits in this book. So, if you are not yet a parent, you will absolutely love what I have to say.
A big reason I wanted to include that in my first paragraph is that before you start your own business you have to know your WHY.

My WHY? Well, it started off as something completely different. My time, my rules, my money, my business. Lots of my...my...my...
Then I got that white dress on and strut beautifully with my pre-preggo body down the aisle. A year later I got pregnant and we took a hard look at my business and if it was worth continuing as I became a mom. Ultimately, we decided... well, I'm sure you wouldn't be reading this book if I had given that up.

My, WHY became my family. The WHY grew, and grew, and grew one last time. (If you are doing the math, yes, we have three kids.) Each member of our family added a whole new layer to what this business looked like... and which each baby, it changed... Drastically.

This book has a lot of what I have learned from observing others in this line of work for the last eleven years. It also has a lot of first-hand lessons-learned stories that might make you feel embarrassed for me at times. Last, of all, it has invaluable information that is going to get you running your full fledge business. AND get that first large paycheck written to you... from you.

Hitting All the Right Notes:
What to Expect in the Following Chapters

Now that we've established why owning a private music studio is the ultimate dream job for us rockstars, it's time to dive into the nitty-gritty details of making it happen.

In the following chapters, we'll cover a range of topics that will help you hit all the right notes in building and growing your private music studio business. Here's a sneak peek of what's to come:

Defining Your Studio's Niche: I'll help you identify your strengths and interests in music and evaluate the local market to establish your unique selling proposition.

Creating a Business Plan: If this sounds like a bore, don't worry. I have some tips on how to spice up this activity. You can't hit the big time without a solid plan. We'll cover everything from crafting a mission statement and business goals to developing a marketing plan and budget.

Managing Finances: Money, money, money - it's what makes the world go round, and your business too. We'll show you how to budget for expenses and revenue, understand taxes and bookkeeping, and seek funding or manage loans.

Building Your Studio Space: It's time to design a space that rocks. We'll help you choose equipment and technology that best fits your needs and create a safe and comfortable environment for students.

Scheduling and Time Management: You want to make sure you're hitting all the right notes, but you also want to make sure you're managing your time effectively. We'll help you develop a scheduling system for your students and manage your time to balance your work and family life.

Creating Curriculum and Lesson Plans: Teaching music is your bread and butter, so we'll help you develop a comprehensive curriculum for your students and create engaging lesson plans that will make them want to come back for more.

Hiring and Managing Instructors and support staff:
You can do it alone, I mean, I did! I did it by myself for over a decade. Half of that was filled with two babies by my side. That being said: You don't have to do it alone. I'll help you identify the skills and qualifications of potential instructors, create job descriptions, and train and manage them effectively.

So, there you have it, folks. It's going to be a wild ride, but with my guidance, you'll be hitting all the right notes in no time. Stay tuned for the following chapters and let's get ready to rock and roll!

Chapter 2

Tuning In

Defining Your Studio's Niche

Finding Your Groove: Identifying Your Strengths and Interests in Music

Alright, my fellow music enthusiasts, let's talk about finding your groove. You know that feeling when you hit the perfect note and everything just clicks? That's the feeling we want to capture when identifying our strengths and interests in music.

Step 1: Digging Deep and Exploring Your Strengths

First things first, grab your favorite instrument (or vocal cords) and start exploring. What comes naturally to you? What do you find yourself constantly coming back to? Take note of the techniques and styles that come easily to you and make a list of your musical strengths.

Step 2: Evaluating Your Musical Background and Education

Next, let's evaluate your musical background and education. Have you been classically trained, or did you learn to play by ear? Have you studied music theory or composition? Understanding your musical education and background will help you identify your unique approach to instruction.

Many teachers out there are fabulous, and never got a music degree. Many teachers out there with music degrees are terrible. Many teachers with music degrees are fantastic... you get the picture right? A music/education/pedagogy degrees are not a prerequisite to being a fantastic teacher.I do think enjoying teaching is a good prerequisite though.

Step 3: Determining Your Best-Suited Instruction

Finally, it's time to determine what type of instruction you're best suited to offer. Are you a whiz with young children, or do you excel at teaching advanced techniques to experienced musicians? Do you specialize in a particular genre or instrument? Knowing your strengths and interests in music will help you build a business that plays to your strengths and sets you apart from the competition.

Step 4: Curriculum

This may take a few years' worth of trial and error to find the best method books for your studio. I started with Bastien and Alfred combos because that's what I started with as a child. In more recent years, I found my perfect match when I decided to switch to Faber, and my own material as a combo. I imagine that's what I will continue to do for many years. Buy the primer and level one book in a few different methods that you are interested in. I will talk about a few more tips in a later chapter.

Let's find our groove and create a private music studio that's as unique as our musical talents. Stay tuned for the next few sections where we'll be evaluating the local market for music instruction and establishing our unique selling proposition.

Finding Your Groove: Evaluating the Local Market for Music Instruction

Alright, musicians, it's time to put on our detective hats and do some research. We need to evaluate the local market for music instruction to make sure we're offering lessons that are in demand and setting ourselves apart from the competition.

Step 1: Scoping Out the Competition

First things first, let's scope out the competition. Who else is offering music instruction in your area? What instruments do they specialize in? What teaching styles do they use? Take a look at their websites, social media pages, and customer reviews to get a sense of what they're offering and how they're perceived by their students.

Step 2: Identifying Gaps in the Market

Next, it's time to identify gaps in the market. Are there particular instruments or genres that aren't currently being offered in your area? Is there a demand for specialized instruction, such as music therapy or performance coaching? Identifying these gaps will help you carve out a unique niche for yourself in the local market.
By fine-tuning your approach to evaluating demand for your music lessons, you can attract the right students and ensure that your business is profitable and sustainable. Keep these tips in mind as you continue to grow and develop your private music studio.

Evaluating Demand and Pricing

Finally, let's evaluate demand and pricing. What are other music instructors charging for lessons in your area? Are there any discounts or package deals being offered? Take a look at online classifieds and community bulletin boards to get a sense of the demand for music instruction in your area.

As you embark on your journey to owning a private music studio, one of the key considerations is to evaluate the demand for your services and set the right pricing. After all, you want to attract students who are serious about learning music, but also make sure you're getting paid what you're worth. Here are some tips for fine-tuning your approach to demand and pricing.

Know Your Market: The first step is to research the market and find out what other music studios in your area are charging for their services. You don't want to price yourself too high or too low. Find a sweet spot that reflects your skills and experience, while also being competitive with your peers.

Define Your Target Audience: Identify the type of students you want to attract and cater your pricing accordingly. Are you targeting beginners, intermediates, or advanced students? Do you specialize in a particular genre or instrument? These factors can influence the demand and pricing for your lessons.

Consider Your Expenses: Running private music studio-incurs costs such as rent, utilities, instruments, and other equipment. Make sure you factor these costs into your pricing so that you are covering your expenses while still making a profit.

Offer Promotions: Sometimes, offering promotions can attract new students and keep existing ones. Offer a discount for students who sign up for multiple lessons or refer a friend. However, be cautious not to offer too many promotions, as it can create an expectation for discounts that may not be sustainable in the long run.

Reevaluate Periodically: Don't set your pricing once and forget about it. Reevaluate your demand and pricing periodically to ensure that it remains competitive and sustainable. Consider factors such as the current economic climate, changes in the music education landscape, and other relevant factors.

With this knowledge in hand, you'll be able to create a private music studio that offers instruction in a unique, in-demand niche at competitive prices. Stay tuned for the next chapter where we'll be establishing our unique selling proposition and branding our business.

Finding Your Rhythm: Determining Your Best-Suited Instruction

It's time to put our expertise to the test and determine what type of instruction we're best suited to offer. After all, we can't just teach any old thing – we need to play to our strengths to create a business that rocks! Most likely you already have an idea of your NICHE instrument, but just in case you are a multi-talented instrument maestro... I think it's best to throw this in here.

Step 1: Analyzing Your Strengths

First up, let's analyze your strengths as a musician and teacher. What instruments are you most comfortable with? What techniques do you excel at teaching? Do you have experience working with children or adults? Knowing your strengths will help you determine what type of instruction you'll be able to offer with confidence.

My Story: Piano is my first love, but in high school, I started to learn guitar. In my early years of teaching, I advertised "Voice Piano and Guitar". I could teach it all, but I wasn't teaching guitar because I loved it. I was teaching it so that I could be a full-service studio in my community. I had students perform at live events, and many came to me to learn guitar. There was just one problem.
I didn't love teaching it.

A few years ago I had a realization. It does me no good to advertise lessons for an instrument that I like, but don't enjoy teaching.
Those students are wonderful, and even if I am competent... our time has better uses. Why not use my precious time to teach instruments I really and truly LOVE to teach?
Now, the piano is my main, and voice is my second offering. I fill most lesson times with piano because of the passion I have for it. That passion rubs off on students and you will see them excel because of it.

Step 2: Identifying Your Interests

Next, it's time to identify your interests in music. Do you have a particular genre or style that you're passionate about? Are there certain instruments that you love to play or teach? Incorporating your interests into your instruction will not only make teaching more enjoyable for you but will also help you attract students who share your musical tastes.

Step 3: Balancing Demand and Interest

Finally, let's balance demand and interest. We want to make sure we're offering instruction that's in demand in our local market, but also that we're passionate about teaching. By analyzing the local market and our own interests, we can find a balance that works for both us and our students.

With this knowledge in hand, you'll be able to create a private music studio that offers instruction in a unique, in-demand niche that plays to your strengths and interests. Stay tuned for the next chapter where we'll be establishing our unique selling proposition and branding our business. Keep on grooving, music makers!

Rhythm Recap

Alright, fellow music lovers, it's time to get down to that re-cap business. Before you can start strumming the strings of success, you need to identify your strengths and establish your unique selling proposition. Write them out. Use the margins if you need to.

Step 1: Identify Your Strengths and Interests in Music

We all have our own unique style and approach to music. Whether you're a classical pianist or a rock guitarist, it's important to identify your strengths and interests to build a business that plays to your strengths. Consider your experience, education, and musical background to determine what type of instruction you're best suited to offer.

Step 2: Evaluate the Local Market for Music Instruction

Just like in music, you need to be aware of what others are playing to stand out from the crowd. Research the local market for music instruction to determine what types of lessons are in demand and who your competition is. Are there already a lot of piano teachers in the area? Maybe you could offer a unique instrument or focus to stand out.

Step 3: Establish Your Unique Selling Proposition

You've identified your strengths and evaluated the local market, now it's time to establish your unique selling proposition. What makes your private music studio stand out from the others? Perhaps you offer a unique genre of music or specialize in working with young children. Whatever it is, make sure to emphasize it in your marketing and branding to differentiate yourself from the rest.

By identifying your strengths and establishing your unique selling proposition, you'll be one step closer to composing your dream job as a private music studio owner. So, rock on and stay tuned for the following chapters where we'll dive deeper into how to build a business plan that hits all the right notes.

Chapter 3

The Beat Goes On

Creating a Business Plan

Don't Be a One-Hit Wonder: The Importance of Having a Solid Business Plan

Ah, the sweet sound of success. But before you can start counting your profits, you need to make sure you're starting off on the right note. And that means having a solid business plan.

Now, I know what you're thinking. "A business plan? That sounds about as fun as practicing scales for hours on end." But trust me, having a plan in place will save you time, money, and headaches down the road.

Here are some key reasons why having a solid business plan is so important:

It helps you define your goals and mission statement: Without a clear understanding of what you want to achieve and what you stand for, it's impossible to make informed decisions and guide your business in the right direction.

It helps you understand your market: Who are your competitors? What are their strengths and weaknesses? What opportunities and challenges exist in your local market? A business plan helps you answer these questions and create a plan of attack.

It helps you budget and manage your finances:Knowing your expenses, revenue streams and projected profits help you make informed decisions about everything from marketing to hiring instructors.

It helps you secure funding: Whether you're seeking a loan or investment, having a a solid business plan is crucial to convincing lenders or investors that you're a sound investment.

So, don't be a one-hit wonder, my fellow music-loving mompreneurs. Take the time to create a comprehensive business plan that sets you up for success. We'll dive deeper into how to create a plan that rocks in the following pages, so stay tuned!

EXAMPLE

BUSINESS PLAN
GREENHOUSE MUSIC

Prepared by:

Delana Green

Executive *Summary*

Who we are

MISSION

At Greenhouse Music, we are dedicated to instilling a love of music in children from all walks of life. We strive to make the learning process an enjoyable one by embracing modern technology and providing affordable education that is both accessible and high quality!

VISION

To be the top-performing online music education platform in the country. To be a quality educational tool for rural schools, and to provide opportunities for kids to expand their learning.

The Product	Online Music Courses
The Leadership	Delana Green-Owner/Operator Darien Green- Support
The Overall Industry	The industry has been controlled by five main players over the past 10 years. However, Greenhouse Music aims to disrupt the industry with a platform that includes gamification, social learning, live classes, and interaction.
The Competitors	The major competitors are: Prodigies Music Simply Piano (Joytunes) Hoffman Academy (free) Pianote and Musiah
The Financial Status	Greenhouse Music is projected to make it's first profit before it's first calendar year after launching is reached. (September 2023 marks one year.
Future Plans	By 2026- The curriculum being used in over 100 schools. By 2030- Greenhouse Music plans to have an APP available as an extension. Created for musical learners. An interactive AI program is implemented into the learning app.

The *Organization*

Behind the name

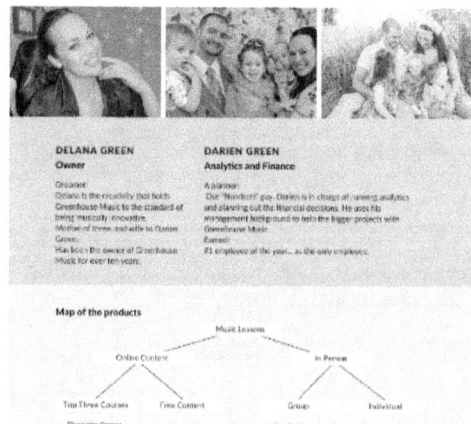

DELANA GREEN
Owner

Dreamer
Delana is the creativity that holds Greenhouse Music to the standard of being musically innovative. Mother of three, and wife to Darien Green. Has been the owner of Greenhouse Music for over ten years.

DARIEN GREEN
Analytics and Finance

A planner
Our "Numbers" guy. Darien is in charge of running analytics and planning out the financial decisions. He uses his management background to help the bigger projects with Greenhouse Music.
Earnest
#1 employee of the year... as the only employee.

Map of the products

Music Lessons

Online Content — In Person

Top Three Courses — Free Content — Group — Individual

Chapter 4

Creating a Business Plan

All right, folks, we've covered some serious ground so far. We've identified our strengths and interests in music, evaluated the local market, and determined our best-suited instruction. But, before we start strumming our guitars in celebration, there's one more important step we need to take - creating a business plan! I'll be one hundred percent honest with you. I did not see the benefit of this until (probably) way *way* later than I should have.

Story time:
I needed funding, I had a huge project and it was NOT going to be cheap.
If you are curious and want an idea of what I was up to, take a look at greenhousemusicak.com
My mentor told me to reach out to the local Economic Development District. Which was basically the SBA (Small Business Association) on steroids for what it could help me with. (Side note: Your local SBA is worth checking out.)

So I reached out and told the director about my project. His first question: "Do you have a business plan written up." at the time I think I tried to convince myself more than him that I did, indeed have one. But, shocker? I did not. The more he talked about the template he had available the more I realized my one-page PDF was not what he had pictured in his head.
So I spent a whole weekend working through a template he provided me with. I ended up with seventeen pages full of answers to questions I hadn't even realized I should be asking.
YIKES.

So here is a great example of "Do what I say and not as I do" (p.s. It's more fun if you say that with solfege "Do")
Corny music jokes aside, let's get to it.

Step 1: Setting Your Goals

To start, let's set some goals. What do you hope to achieve with your private music studio? Do you want to become the go-to teacher for a particular instrument or genre? Are you hoping to expand your business to multiple locations? Setting specific, measurable goals will help keep you on track and focused on what you want to achieve.

Step 2: Identifying Your Target Audience

Next, it's important to identify your target audience. Who are you hoping to attract to your studio? Are you aiming to work with young children, teenagers, or adults? Understanding your target audience will help you tailor your instruction, marketing, and pricing to meet their needs.

Step 3: Establishing Your Unique Selling Proposition

Now it's time to establish your unique selling proposition (USP). What sets your studio apart from the competition? Is it your years of experience, your innovative teaching style, or your specialization in a particular genre or instrument? Your USP is what will attract potential students to your studio and keep them coming back for more.

Step 4: Developing Your Marketing Strategy

Finally, we need to develop a marketing strategy that will help us reach our target audience and communicate our USP. Will you advertise through social media, flyers, or word-of-mouth? How will you price your lessons and what promotions or discounts will you offer? Answering these questions will help you develop a comprehensive marketing plan that will help your business grow.

Creating a business plan may not be the most glamorous aspect of starting a private music studio, but it's essential for ensuring your success. Keep on grooving, music makers, and stay tuned for the next chapter where we'll be diving into branding your business.

3 Marketing Tips

FOR SMALL BUSINESS

1 UNDERSTAND YOUR CUSTOMER

2 ENGAGE ON SOCIAL MEDIA

3 KEEP UP WITH THE TRENDS

Chapter 5

Creating a Missions Statement

All right, time to get down to the nitty-gritty of this dream job. Before you start jamming out with your new music studio, it's important to craft a mission statement and set some business goals.

First things first, let's talk mission *statement*. Think of this as your studio's theme song. It should be catchy, and memorable, and communicate what you're all about. Are you all about fostering creativity and self-expression? Or maybe you're all about helping students achieve their musical dreams. Whatever it is, make it clear and concise so that even someone who's tone-deaf can understand.

Next up, business goals. These are like the notes that make up a melody. They should be specific, measurable, and achievable. Do you want to have a certain number of students enrolled within a certain timeframe? Or maybe you want to expand your studio to offer more types of lessons? Whatever your goals, make sure they align with your mission statement and are in line with what you want to achieve.

Remember, creating a mission statement and business goals isn't just a one-time thing. Just like a great song, they may evolve over time as your studio grows and changes. So don't be afraid to revisit and revise them as needed.

Now let's get out there and make some music (and some money)!

5 QUESTIONS

Before branding your business

WHAT MAKES YOUR BUSINESS UNIQUE

WHAT IS YOUR MISSION STATEMENT

WHAT ARE YOUR VALUES

WHO IS YOUR AUDIENCE

WHAT IS YOUR MESSAGE

Chapter 6

Marketing and Budgeting

Alrighty folks, it's time to bring out the big guns – we're talking about marketing and budgeting!

Marketing is like the hook that gets people interested in your music. It's important to have a solid plan in place to promote your studio and attract potential students. Start by identifying your target audience – whom are you trying to reach? Young kids just starting out, or more advanced musicians looking to fine-tune their skills? Once you know whom you're trying to reach, you can tailor your marketing efforts to appeal to them. This could include social media ads, flyers around town, or even partnering with local schools or music shops.

Now, let's talk budget. Money may not grow on trees, but that doesn't mean you can't make it rain. It's important to set a budget for your marketing efforts so you don't overspend and end up in *treble*. Start by determining how much you can realistically afford to spend each month on marketing. From there, you can allocate funds to different tactics, such as paying for social media ads or printing flyers.

Remember, marketing and budgeting are two sides of the same coin. You need to invest in your marketing efforts in order to attract new students and make your music studio a success. But at the same time, you need to be smart about how you're spending your money to ensure you're not going over budget.

So get ready to put your marketing skills to the test – and hopefully, you'll be singing all the way to the bank!

Chapter 7

Growth and Sustainability

Alright folks, it's time to start thinking big – we're talking about planning for growth and sustainability!

Now that you've got your music studio up and running, it's time to start thinking about how you can take things to the next level. Do you want to expand your offerings to include more instruments or genres? Or maybe you want to hire additional instructors to help you keep up with demand?

Whatever your goals may be, it's important to have a plan in place to ensure sustainable growth. This means setting realistic targets for revenue and enrollment and putting processes in place to ensure you're able to meet demand while still delivering high-quality instruction.

One key strategy for sustainable growth is to invest in your instructors. By providing ongoing training and support, you can ensure your team is equipped to deliver the best possible instruction to your students. This will help you retain students and attract new ones, helping you achieve your growth targets.

Another key strategy is to stay connected with your community. This could mean attending local events or sponsoring community music programs. By staying engaged with your community, you can build a strong reputation and attract new students to your studio.

So get ready to dream big and plan for success! With the right strategy in place, there's no limit to what you can achieve with your music studio.

MY GOAL:

STOP
DOING

DO
LESS OF

KEEP
DOING

Goal Planner

The Goal:

The Strategy:

Steps to Take: **Other Notes**

Chapter 8

Scale Up - Managing Finances

Budgeting for your business expenses and revenue

All right, it's time to put on your finance hat and get serious about managing your money. As much as we all love music, at the end of the day, your music studio is a business, and that means you need to keep a close eye on your finances.

First things first: you need to create a budget. This means figuring out all of your expenses, from rent and utilities to instructor salaries and equipment costs. Once you know how much you're spending, you can start to figure out how much revenue you need to bring in to cover those costs and make a profit.

But creating a budget is just the beginning. You also need to track your income and expenses throughout the year to make sure you're on track to meet your financial goals. This means keeping track of all your invoices, receipts, and other financial records.

To help manage your finances, you may want to consider investing in accounting software or hiring a professional accountant. They can help you create a budget, track your finances, and prepare your tax returns, saving you time and stress.

Another important aspect of financial management is planning for the future. This means setting aside money for emergencies, investing in equipment or facilities upgrades, and planning for long-term growth.

So don't be afraid to get your hands dirty with some number-crunching. By staying on top of your finances, you'll be better equipped to grow your business and achieve your goals.

Understanding taxes and bookkeeping

Welcome to the chapter that is guaranteed to make your eyes cross and your head spin - Managing Finances! But don't worry, we'll keep it as fun and comical as possible.

Now, we know that talking about finances isn't exactly the most thrilling topic, but it's crucial to the success of your music studio. It's important to understand how to manage your money effectively, so that you can avoid any financial pitfalls down the road.

First things first, let's talk about budgeting. You need to create a budget for your business, including all of your expenses and projected revenue. This will help you stay on track and make sure you don't overspend. And trust us, overspending is as dangerous as a drummer with a loose cymbal!

Next, let's talk about taxes. Oh, the dreaded "T" word. We know it's not the most exciting topic, but it's important to understand how taxes work for your business. Make sure you keep track of all your income and expenses throughout the year so that when tax season rolls around, you're ready to go.

I have been a huge fan of Turbo Tax home and business. I have been able to get more efficient every year, taking less time to file my taxes. If you use Quickbooks (I don't) it integrates even more.

And finally, bookkeeping. We know, we know, it's not the most glamorous task, but keeping accurate records of your finances is crucial. It helps you keep track of your income and expenses, and allows you to analyze your financial health. Plus, it'll make your accountant very happy. As a music teacher, my favorite tool has been My Music Staff. It easily keeps track of my expenses and gives me the report at the end of the year.

So there you have it - managing finances in a nutshell. Don't worry if it all seems overwhelming at first. With a little bit of practice and patience, you'll become a financial wizard in no time!

Seeking funding and managing loans

Ahoy there, mateys! It's time to talk about the not-so-fun side of running your own music studio - finances! Don't worry, we'll make this as fun and entertaining as possible.

In this chapter, we'll cover two important topics: seeking funding and managing loans. As much as we'd like to think that our music studio will be an instant success, the reality is that it may take some time to turn a profit. That's where funding comes in. First, let's talk about seeking funding. There are a few options available to you, such as:

Personal savings:If you've been saving up for thisventure, this could be the perfect time to dip into your savings to help get your music studio off the ground. It's not needed if you have no overhead cost. For instance, I started this business with $0 at nineteen years old. I was teaching out of my parents living room on my electric piano. No rent, no overhead worries. It's possible to start with nothing.

Friends and family:If you have supportive friends and family who believe in your dream, they may be willing to invest in your business. This comes down to a great business plan. If you don't have your business plan solid and ready to present, there isn't that strong of a case for investors.

Business loans:You can also look into getting a businessloan from a bank or other financial institution. However, before you go down the route of a loan, see if it's possible to start your business off debt-free. I've run my business for over a decade, debt-free and there is some power that I feel being able to say that.

No matter which option you choose, it's important to have a solid plan in place to convince potential investors or lenders that your music studio is a sound investment.

Now, let's talk about managing loans. If you do take out a business loan, it's important to understand the terms and conditions, including the interest rate and repayment schedule. Make sure you have a plan in place to manage your loan payments and ensure that you're able to keep up with them.

It's also important to keep detailed records of your finances, including all income and expenses. This will make it easier come tax season, as you'll have all the necessary information to file your taxes accurately.

Managing finances may not be the most exciting part of owning a music studio, but it's crucial for your business's success. So, don't be afraid to ask for help from a financial advisor or accountant if you need it. With proper planning and management, your music studio can continue to grow and thrive for years to come.

INCOME

EXPENSE

_____

_____

_____

TOTAL INCOME

TOTAL EXPENSE

_____

_____

Chapter 9

Sound Check - Building Your Studio Space

Designing a functional and inspiring studio space

Alrighty, let's get started on Chapter 9! It's time to talk about everyone's favorite part of owning a private music studio - building the studio space!

First things first, let's talk about functionality. You want your studio space to be organized and efficient so you can maximize your time and energy. Make sure you have all the necessary equipment and tools within reach and create a layout that allows for easy movement between different areas of the studio.

But functionality doesn't mean sacrificing style, honey. You want your studio to look inspiring and welcoming, so your students feel excited to learn and grow. Choose colors and decor that reflect your personal style and the vibe you want to create. Maybe you're into bright and bold colors, or maybe you prefer a more minimalist and modern aesthetic. Whatever your style, make sure it's reflected in your studio space.

Now, let's talk about the most important part of any music studio - the sound. Make sure you invest in high-quality soundproofing materials, so your students can focus on their music without any outside distractions. You don't want to be hearing the neighbor's dog barking during a piano lesson, trust me.

Finally, don't forget to add some personal touches to your studio space. Maybe you want to display some of your favorite musical instruments or artwork on the walls. Or maybe you want to create a cozy corner with some pillows and blankets where your students can relax and take a break during their lessons. Whatever it is, make sure it's something that reflects your personality and makes your studio feel like home.

There you have it, folks! With these tips, you'll be well on your way to designing a functional and inspiring studio space that's perfect for you and your students. Now, let's get back to making beautiful music together!

Choosing equipment and technology

It's time to talk about one of the most exciting parts of building your private music studio - choosing the equipment and technology. Now, don't let the technical jargon intimidate you. We'll break it down in a way that even your grandma can understand.

First up, let's talk about the essentials. You'll need instruments, and if you plan to do recordings or are a performance-based studio, you will also need amplifiers, microphones, and speakers, depending on the type of music you'll be teaching. But don't forget about the smaller things too, such as music stands, sheet music, and instrument stands. And let's not forget about the most important piece of equipment in any music studio - the coffee machine!
(p.s. This can totally be a business write-off.)

Now, let's talk about the fancy stuff - technology. You don't have to be a tech wizard to understand this. Just think about what technology will help you be more efficient and effective in your teaching. Maybe you want to invest in software that helps you create and organize lesson plans, or maybe you want to use a digital audio workstation for recording and editing music.

But wait, there's more! Don't forget about the fun stuff. You know, the things that make your studio stand out from the rest. Maybe you want to install some funky lighting or add some cool artwork to the walls. Or maybe you want to create a chill-out area where your students can relax and jam out between lessons. Whatever it is, make sure it's something that reflects your personality and makes your studio unique.

And remember, choosing equipment and technology doesn't have to break the bank. You can find great deals on used equipment and there are plenty of free software options available online. So, don't let the cost hold you back from creating the music studio of your dreams.

Choosing equipment and instruments for your private music studio doesn't have to cost you an arm and a leg, my friends. In fact, with a little bit of creativity and resourcefulness, you can set up a fully functional studio without breaking the bank. Here are some tips to help you choose equipment and instruments on a budget:

Set a budget: Before you start shopping, decide how much you can afford to spend. This will help you narrow down your options and avoid overspending.

Go used: Buying used equipment and instruments is a great way to save money. Check out local classifieds, music stores, and online marketplaces like eBay and Craigslist. You might be surprised at what you can find.

Rent or borrow: If you only need a piece of equipment or instrument for a short period of time, consider renting or borrowing instead of buying. This can save you a lot of money in the long run.

Prioritize: Make a list of the equipment and instruments you need and prioritize them based on what's most important. This will help you focus on the essentials and avoid overspending on unnecessary items.

Shop around: Don't settle for the first deal you find. Shop around and compare prices at different stores and online retailers. You might be able to find a better deal or a promotion that will help you save money.

Negotiate: Don't be afraid to negotiate the price. If you're buying used equipment or instruments, the seller might be willing to lower the price if you ask.

Look for sales: Keep an eye out for sales and promotions at music stores and online retailers. You might be able to snag a great deal on the equipment or instrument you need.

DIY: If you're handy, consider building your own equipment or modifying existing equipment to suit your needs. This can be a fun and cost-effective way to set up your studio.

Remember, setting up a private music studio on a budget is all about being resourceful and creative. With a little bit of effort, you can create a functional and inspiring studio without spending a fortune.

There you have it, folks! With these tips, you'll be well on your way to choosing the perfect equipment and technology for your private music studio. And who knows, maybe one day you'll even become a tech wizard yourself!

Creating a safe and comfortable environment for students

Hey there, rockstars and divas! It's time to talk about creating a safe and comfortable environment for your music students. After all, a great studio space is more than just cool equipment and funky lighting. It's a place where students can feel supported, inspired, and free to explore their musical passions.

First things first, let's talk about safety. This might not be the most exciting topic, but it's definitely an important one. Make sure your studio space is free of hazards like tripping hazards, loose cords, and unstable equipment. You don't want your students to hurt themselves while rocking out! And don't forget about fire safety too. Make sure you have working smoke detectors and fire extinguishers on hand. Safety first, my friends!

Next up, let's talk about comfort. You want your students to feel at home in your studio space. Make sure you have comfortable chairs and a space heater or air conditioner to regulate the temperature. You might also want to provide some snacks and drinks for your students. After all, playing music can be hungry work!

But comfort goes beyond just physical comfort. You want your students to feel emotionally comfortable too. Make sure you create a welcoming and inclusive environment where everyone feels respected and valued. I will never forget going about my regular lesson procedure with a very sweet eight-year-old boy. I was having him repeat a difficult section like I normally do when he burst into tears. I felt terrible. Turns out, his grandfather had just passed away. I think of that story way too often, to remind myself that every child is carrying something into their lessons with me. Sometimes it's light, sometimes it's heavy. I always tell parents in my intake session that if the kiddo is having a hard day, the best thing is to let me know. This way I can focus on some light activities and not drilling those arpeggios.

Encourage your students to be themselves and express themselves freely through music. And don't forget to give them plenty of positive feedback and encouragement. We all need a little confidence boost from time to time!

Last but not least, don't forget to have some fun! Playing music should be a joyful and exciting experience. Create a playful and creative atmosphere in your studio space. Maybe you want to decorate with fun posters or add some plants to liven up the space. Whatever it is, make sure it reflects your personality and makes your students feel happy and inspired.

So there you have it, folks! By creating a safe, comfortable, and playful environment for your music students, you'll help them unlock their full potential and achieve their musical dreams. Keep on rockin'!

Chapter 10

Time Signature - Scheduling and Time Management

Developing a scheduling system for your students

All right, folks, it's time to talk about everyone's favorite topic...time management! cue eye roll I know, I know, it's not the most exciting part of owning a private music studio. But trust me, it's super important if you want to keep your sanity and your students happy. So let's talk about scheduling and time management.

First things first, let's talk about scheduling. When it comes to scheduling lessons, you want to make sure you're organized and efficient. Set specific times for each lesson and make sure your students know what their schedule is. If you have multiple students, create a schedule that works for everyone. And don't forget to leave some buffer time between lessons in case things run over.

But scheduling isn't just about lessons. You also need to schedule time for administrative tasks like billing, marketing, and bookkeeping. Set aside specific times each week to take care of these tasks, so they don't pile up and overwhelm you.

Now let's talk about time management. When you're running a private music studio, it's easy to get bogged down in administrative tasks and forget about the fun stuff like playing music! So make sure you prioritize your time and set boundaries. Don't let administrative tasks take over your entire day. Instead, schedule specific times for these tasks and stick to them. And don't be afraid to say no to things that don't align with your goals and priorities.

Another important part of time management is taking breaks. Yes, breaks! It might sound counterintuitive, but taking breaks can actually make you more productive in the long run. Take a few minutes to stretch, grab a snack, or even play some music for yourself. Your brain will thank you!

Last but not least, remember to be flexible. Things don't always go according to plan, and that's okay. If a student needs to reschedule a lesson or if an unexpected task comes up, roll with it. If improv classes are provided in your area, TAKE THEM. I can't tell you how many times the phrase "Yes, and" is used in my lessons. Especially with the littles who want to tell you all about the cool bug they found at recess. Don't let the little things stress you out. Roll with it, and be ready to adjust.

So there you have it, folks. Scheduling and time management might not be the most exciting topics, but they're crucial if you want to run a successful private music studio. Stay organized, set boundaries, take breaks, and be flexible. You've got this!

Managing your time and balancing your work and family life

This is a tough one for me, we're going to talk about a topic that is near and dear to the hearts of many of us: managing our time and balancing our work and family lives. It's a delicate dance, but it can be done!

First things first, let's talk about setting boundaries. When you're running a private music studio, it can be easy to let your work bleed into your personal life. But it's important to set boundaries and separate the two. Make sure you have specific work hours and stick to them. When you're not working, try to disconnect and focus on your family and personal life. I am a mom to three little girls. As I am writing this, they are five, three, and one. You know, the tough ages, but also the ones that you don't want to miss. This year, because of a massive project I was working on, I found I was working sixty hours a week. Likely more. My husband (we joke that he is my manager) is the schedule and numbers guy. I am creative. So he built a schedule for me to follow. My work day begins at ten in the morning. From ten to one I work on the computer and any tasks related to it. At one, I take a lunch break and eat. At two, I teach until six.

Trust me, I resisted at first, but this made it so that the weekends could be spent as a family. I don't want to work so much that I miss the little years before my kids start school. My guess is if you have kids, you want to be there for it as well. If you don't have kids, this is still a great habit to get into. Create a schedule, find the peak times that you have the most energy, and use that for the things that require the most. This leads me to my next point.

Another important part of time management is prioritization. You only have so many hours in the day, so it's important to prioritize the tasks that are most important. Make a list of your daily tasks and rank them in order of importance. Focus on the most important tasks first and work your way down the list. This will help you stay focused and avoid getting overwhelmed.

But what about those unexpected tasks that pop up? Well, that's where flexibility comes in. Life is unpredictable, and sometimes things don't go according to plan. But if you're able to be flexible and adapt to changes, you'll be much better equipped to handle whatever comes your way.

One way to manage your time more effectively is to delegate tasks. If you have a spouse, partner, or older children, consider asking them to help with tasks like picking up supplies or managing your social media accounts. This will free up some of your time and help you achieve a better balance between your work and family lives.

Finally, don't forget to take care of yourself. When you're busy juggling work and family responsibilities, it can be easy to forget about self-care. But taking care of yourself is crucial if you want to avoid burnout and maintain your energy and motivation. Make sure you schedule time for activities that make you happy and relaxed, like exercise, reading, or spending time with friends.

Balancing your work and family lives can be a challenge, but with some careful planning, prioritization, and delegation, you can find the balance that works for you. And don't forget to take care of yourself along the way!

Delegating tasks and outsourcing

I've probably told the following story about ten times in the last few months. I had a former piano teacher enroll her kids in my studio. She had been teaching for twenty years and had four children for me to teach. After getting to know the family, I was just in awe of her ability to "mom" and teach. I asked her (as someone in the thick of mom/work life) "How did you do it." She said very frankly: "Outsource, and delegate." It hit me like a brick. Hence why I love this story. Not only has it been an honor to teach her kids, but I also look at them and see a reflection of what my life might look like soon. Knowing that it doesn't all have to fall on one person can be so freeing. This isn't a parenting book but that is one thing that I really want to drive home. Delegate. If you need someone to watch your kiddos while you teach, sweet! Find a mommy helper that can come and play with them in another room. If you HATE all things bookkeeping, see if you can find someone to help. Hate the marketing side? Get a Canva account... Well, get a Canva account.

Delegating involves assigning tasks to other people, whether it's a family member, friend, or employee. This can help you free up some of your time and focus on the tasks that require your specific expertise.

When delegating, it's important to choose the right person for the job. Make sure the person you choose has the necessary skills and experience to handle the task. It's also important to communicate clearly and provide instructions and guidance to ensure the task is completed correctly.

Another option for managing your workload is outsourcing. Outsourcing involves hiring a third-party company or individual to handle specific tasks for you. This can be a great option if you don't have the skills or resources to handle certain tasks in-house.

When outsourcing, it's important to do your research and choose a reputable and reliable service provider. Make sure to communicate your expectations clearly and establish deadlines and milestones to ensure the work is completed on time and to your satisfaction.

Delegating and outsourcing can be valuable tools for managing your time and workload, but it's important to use them wisely. Don't delegate or outsource tasks that require your specific expertise or that are essential to your business's success. It's also important to maintain control and oversight over the tasks being delegated or outsourced to ensure they meet your standards.

In summary, delegating tasks and outsourcing can help you manage your time and workload more effectively. By choosing the right people or service providers and communicating clearly, you can free up more time to focus on the tasks that require your specific expertise. But remember, it's important to use these tools wisely and maintain control and oversight over the tasks being delegated or outsourced.

Chapter 11 Key Signature

Creating Curriculum and Lesson Plans

Developing a comprehensive curriculum for your students

Hey there, music mavens! Welcome to Chapter 11, where we'll be talking about creating curriculum and lesson plans. I know, I know, it doesn't sound like the most exciting topic but trust me, it's important! First things first, when developing a curriculum, you want to make sure it's comprehensive. That means covering all the important topics your students need to know. But let's be real, who has time for that? I mean, do your students really need to know the history of the kazoo? Probably not.

So, instead of trying to cover everything under the sun, focus on the most important topics and skills your students need to learn. And hey, if you have extra time, throw in some fun stuff too. Who doesn't love a lesson on how to play the kazoo?

When creating lesson plans, it's important to keep things fresh and engaging. Let's face it, no one wants to sit through a boring lesson. So, think outside the box! Maybe you could teach your students how to play a song using only kitchen utensils. Or have them compose their own original piece using random objects found around the house.

Don't forget to incorporate plenty of breaks and snacks into your lessons. After all, a hungry or restless student is not a happy student. Trust me, I speak from experience.

In summary, when creating a curriculum and lesson plans, focus on the most important topics and skills your students need to learn, but don't be afraid to throw in some fun and creative elements. Keep things engaging and don't forget to take breaks and provide snacks. And remember, the history of the kazoo can wait.

Creating engaging and effective lesson plans

Here we'll be talking about creating engaging and effective lesson plans. I know what you're thinking, "Lesson plans? Boring!" But fear not, my friends. With a little creativity, we can make lesson planning as fun as a kazoo solo.

First off, let's talk about making lessons engaging. We've all been there, sitting in a class and struggling to stay awake while the teacher drones on and on. Don't be that teacher! Make your lessons fun and interactive. Maybe you could have your students create their own instruments out of recycled materials and then use them in a class performance. Or teach them how to play a song using only their feet! (Just make sure they're wearing socks, please.)

But let's not forget about the effectiveness of our lessons. Sure, playing the kazoo is fun, but we also want our students to learn something. So, make sure your lessons have clear objectives and are designed to help your students achieve specific goals. And remember, not every student learns the same way. Some may be more visual learners, while others may learn better through hands-on activities. So, try to incorporate a variety of teaching methods to reach all your students.

Now, let's talk about the nitty-gritty of lesson planning. Make sure you have a clear structure and plan for each lesson. Start with an introduction, move on to the main content, and end with a summary or activity to reinforce what was learned. And don't forget to keep track of what you've taught so you can build on it in future lessons.

In summary, creating engaging and effective lesson plans doesn't have to be a drag. Use your creativity to make lessons fun and interactive, but also ensure they have clear objectives and a structure. And remember, not every student learns the same way, so incorporate a variety of teaching methods to reach all your students. Now go forth and make some music!

LESSON FOCUS AND GOALS

MATERIALS NEEDED

LEARNING OBJECTIVES

STRUCTURE / ACTIVITY

Incorporating music theory and performance skills into lessons

Welcome, fellow musicians, to Chapter 11 part two, where we'll be talking about incorporating music theory and performance skills into lessons. Don't worry, I won't bore you with a lecture on music theory, but I will make you laugh with some musical puns.

Now, when it comes to music theory, it can be a bit of a snooze-fest. But fear not, there are ways to make it more interesting. For example, you could use food analogies to explain musical concepts. You know, like how a chord progression is like a pizza - you have different toppings (chords) that come together to create a delicious melody. Or how the different sections of a song are like a three-course meal - you have your appetizer (intro), main course (verse and chorus), and dessert (outro).

But let's not forget about performance skills. After all, what's the point of learning music theory if you can't perform it? One way to incorporate performance skills into lessons is to have your students practice playing in different styles. For example, have them play a classical piece, followed by a jazz tune, and then a pop song. Or challenge them to perform a piece with a certain emotion, like playing a sad song while pretending to be happy.

No lesson would be complete without a little bit of humor. Try incorporating silly challenges into your lessons, like having your students play a song using only their noses (just make sure they wash their hands first!). Or have them play a song blindfolded, with their instrument upside down, or while standing on one foot.

In summary, incorporating music theory and performance skills into lessons doesn't have to be a snooze-fest. Use food analogies to explain musical concepts, challenge your students to play in different styles, and add a bit of humor to keep things interesting. And remember, just like a good melody, a good lesson has ups and downs, highs and lows, and hopefully, a satisfying resolution.

Chapter 12: Rhythm Section
Hiring and Managing Instructors

Identifying the skills and qualifications of potential instructors

Welcome to the final chapter of "Composing Your Dream Job"! Today, we're going to be talking about how to identify the skills and qualifications of potential instructors. Now, I know what you're thinking - "How do I know if someone is qualified to teach music?"

Well, the first step is to make sure they can actually play an instrument. I mean, you don't want to hire someone who's never touched a guitar before, right? And let's be honest, if they can't even play "Hot Cross Buns" on the recorder, they probably shouldn't be teaching anyone else how to play.

But it's not just about playing an instrument. You want someone who's knowledgeable about music theory and can communicate it effectively to students. So, ask potential instructors about their education and experience in music theory. And if they start spewing out terms like "modal interchange" and "double harmonic minor scale", just nod your head and pretend like you know what they're talking about.

Of course, you also want someone who's passionate about teaching and can connect with their students. So, ask potential instructors about their teaching philosophy and how they handle difficult students. And if they mention anything about "bringing out the inner musician" or "nurturing the creative soul", you know you've found a winner.

In summary, when it comes to identifying the skills and qualifications of potential instructors, make sure they can actually play an instrument, have knowledge of music theory, and are passionate about teaching. And remember, if all else fails, just make sure they can at least play "Hot Cross Buns" on the recorder.

Creating job descriptions and interviewing candidates

Now, I know what you're thinking -
"How hard can it be to interview someone for a music teaching position?"

Well, let me tell you, it's not as easy as it sounds. First off, you need to come up with a catchy job description that will attract the right candidates. Something like, "Wanted: Rockstar Music Instructor to Join Our Band of Misfits". Trust me, you'll get way more applicants that way. Okay, it's not as simple as that. As a parent, when I hire someone, it has to be someone I would trust to teach my own kids. Skill set, and comfortability level both play a huge part.

But once you have a pool of potential candidates, it's time to start the interviews. And let me tell you, these interviews can be a real jam session. You'll want to ask questions like, "If you were a musical instrument, which one would you be and why?" or "What's your go-to karaoke song?"

Don't forget to throw in a few curveballs, like asking them to play a song on the spoons or sing "The Wheels on the Bus" in a heavy metal voice. Hey, if they can't handle the pressure of a silly interview question, how are they going to handle teaching a room full of kids how to play "Mary Had a Little Lamb"?

In summary, when it comes to creating job descriptions and interviewing candidates, don't be afraid to get creative and have a little fun. After all, you're building a team of music-loving misfits, so you want to make sure you find the right fit. And remember, if all else fails, just ask them to sing "The Wheels on the Bus" in a heavy metal voice. It's a real game-changer.

Training and managing instructors

Now, managing a group of musicians can be a bit like herding cats. They're creative, unpredictable, and sometimes a little moody (or maybe that's just me. But don't worry, with a little bit of patience and a lot of coffee, you can turn your team of musical misfits into a well-oiled machine.

First things first, you need to make sure your instructors are trained and up-to-date on the latest teaching techniques. This means you might have to sit them down for some training sessions and let's face it, getting a group of musicians to sit still for more than five minutes is like trying to get a toddler to eat broccoli. So, make sure you have plenty of snacks and maybe even some adult beverages on hand.

Once your instructors are trained, it's time to manage them. This means scheduling lessons, dealing with parents, and making sure your instructors show up on time. Now, I know what you're thinking, "But how do I get my instructors to show up on time?" Well, my friend, you have to speak their language. Instead of saying "Be here at 3 pm", say "We need you to be here at 3 pm to jam with the coolest group of kids in town". Trust me, they'll show up early and ready to rock.

If all else fails, just remember that employees are like plants. They need a little bit of love, a little bit of water, and a whole lot of sunshine. So, make sure you give your instructors plenty of praise and recognition, and they'll grow into the rockstars you always knew they could be.

In summary, when it comes to training and managing your music instructors, it's all about finding the right balance between structure and creativity. And if all else fails, just remember that musicians are like cats, they'll do what they want, when they want, but if you give them a little bit of love and attention, they'll always come back to you.

Chapter 13: The Band
Collaborating with Other Music Professionals

Networking with other music professionals in your area

As a music studio owner, it's important to not only connect with other musicians but also with those outside of the music industry. If there is no opportunity in your area to meet with other professionals... create one. I started a group for Mom business owners, and it's been so nice to be able to talk with other women in the same boat as me. We meet for coffee (virtual and in person), partner together for giveaways, and did I mention coffee? We do a lot of that.

Networking with non-music professionals can open up new opportunities for your studio, such as partnering with local schools or community organizations. It can also help you learn about different business strategies and gain insight into marketing and branding techniques. I also personally found that the children of other professionals make great students.

When it comes to networking with other music professionals, the opportunities are endless. You can attend local concerts and music festivals, participate in music industry events, and even connect with other music studios in your area. Collaborating with other musicians can also lead to new creative ideas and potential collaborations in the future. Let's be honest, networking can be daunting, especially if you're an introverted musician. So, here are a few tips to make networking a little less scary:

Be authentic- don't try to be someone you're not. People can spot a fake from a mile away, and it can be a major turn-off. This includes in person, and social media posts.

Listen more than you talk- when you're meeting someone new, ask questions and really listen to their answers. It shows that you're interested in what they have to say and can help build a connection.

Follow up- after meeting someone new, make sure to follow up with an email or a quick message on social media. It shows that you're serious about building a relationship.

In summary, collaborating and networking with other music and non-music professionals can help grow your music studio and bring new opportunities. So, get out there, be yourself, and make some new connections!

Collaborating with musicians and performers for events and performances

As a music studio owner, you have the opportunity to organize events and performances for your students and the community. Collaborating with other musicians and performers can add variety and excitement to these events, making them more memorable and enjoyable for everyone involved.

When it comes to collaborating with other musicians and performers, there are a few things to keep in mind:

1. **Choose collaborators carefully**- make sure to choose musicians and performers whose style and skill level complement your students and the event. It's also important to make sure they're reliable and professional.
2. **Communicate clearly**- when collaborating with other musicians and performers, make sure to communicate clearly about expectations, rehearsal schedules, and performance details. This will help ensure everyone is on the same page and the event runs smoothly.
3. **Be open to new ideas**- collaborating with other musicians and performers can bring new and exciting ideas to the table. Don't be afraid to try new things and experiment with different styles and genres.
4. **Give credit where credit is due**- when collaborating with other musicians and performers, make sure to give credit where credit is due. This includes crediting them in event programs and promotional materials, and acknowledging their contributions during the performance.

In summary, collaborating with other musicians and performers can add variety and excitement to events and performances, making them more memorable and enjoyable for everyone involved. Just remember to choose collaborators carefully, communicate clearly, be open to new ideas, and give credit where credit is due.

Establishing partnerships with local businesses and organizations

As a business owner, you have the opportunity to collaborate with local businesses and organizations to create mutually beneficial partnerships. This can help you reach new audiences, promote your studio, and create new opportunities for your students.

When it comes to establishing partnerships, there are a few things to keep in mind:

Identify potential partners- think about businesses and organizations in your a community that aligns with your values and mission. This could include music stores, schools, community centers, and more.

Reach out and make connections - once you've identified potential partners, reach out and make connections. Attend networking events, send emails, and schedule meetings to discuss potential partnership opportunities.

Be creative- there are many different ways to collaborate with local businesses and organizations. You could offer music lessons or performances at their location, create joint marketing campaigns, or offer discounts to each other's customers.

Communicate clearly- when establishing a partnership, make sure to communicate clearly about expectations, goals, and responsibilities. This will help ensure that both parties are on the same page and the partnership runs smoothly.

Maintain the relationship- once you've established a partnership, make sure to maintain the relationship by staying in touch, providing updates on your studio's activities, and continuing to explore new opportunities for collaboration.

In summary, establishing partnerships with local businesses and organizations can help you reach new audiences, promote your studio, and create new opportunities for your students. Just remember to identify potential partners, reach out and make connections, be creative, communicate clearly, and maintain the relationship.

Chapter 14: Crescendo
Building Your Reputation and Brand
Creating a brand identity and message

Creating a strong brand identity is essential for any business, including your music studio. But don't worry, building your brand doesn't have to be boring or stuffy. In fact, let's jazz things up a bit with some fun and creative tips!

Get creative with your branding - who says music studios have to be all about black-and-white logos and boring fonts? Get creative with your branding! Use bright colors, funky designs, and bold statements that really capture your unique style.

Be consistent- once you've established your brand identity, make sure to be consistent across all platforms. This includes your website, social media, and any promotional materials. Consistency helps to build recognition and trust with your audience.

Focus on your message- what do you want your music studio to stand for? Whether it's promoting music education or creating a fun and welcoming environment for students, make sure your message is clear and consistent.

Leverage social media- social media is a powerful tool for building your brand and reaching new audiences. Use platforms like Instagram and TikTok to showcase your studio's personality and connect with potential students.

Get involved in the community- building a strong reputation and brand isn't just about online presence. Get involved in local events, volunteer in the community, and showcase your studio's talents through performances and concerts. So far the best advertising for me has been when I give free classes for kids in the community once a month. I meet other parents, they ask questions, they bring friends, and I build authority in my community. People know my business very well now because of the amount of time I spend in the community.

In summary, building your reputation and brand doesn't have to be boring or stuffy. Get creative, be consistent, focus on your message, leverage social media, and get involved in the community to really build your brand and stand out in the music education industry. Find ways to become the leading authority in your community so that you are the first that comes to mind. Let's make your brand crescendo to new heights!

Building an online presence and using social media

In this digital age, having an online presence is crucial for any business, including your music studio. But let's face it, social media can be overwhelming and confusing. It's also a part time job in itself. This is one area I highly recommend setting boundaries in. So, let's spice things up with some fun and creative tips!

1. **Choose the right platform-** not all social media platforms are created equal. Don't spread yourself too thin, focus on the platforms that are most relevant to your audience and that you can consistently maintain.
2. **Be human-** social media is all about being social! Don't be afraid to show your studio's personality and connect with your followers. Share behind-the-scenes glimpses, fun memes, and even the occasional dad joke.

3. **Engage with your followers**- don't just post and run. Take the time to engage with your followers by responding to comments, sharing user-generated content, and hosting Q&A sessions. This helps to build a sense of community and loyalty among your followers.

4. **Create engaging content**- social media is a noisyplace, so make sure your content stands out. Share performance videos, student success stories, and even fun challenges or contests that get your followers involved.

5. **Don't neglect the basics**- make sure your social mediaprofiles are complete with a clear bio, profile picture, and contact information. And remember, consistency is key - make sure to post regularly and at optimal times.

6. **Build the email list now**- I can't stress this enough.If you are focused more on your social media follower count than you are on your newsletter count, you are missing out on a huge opportunity. I use Flodesk and it's been wonderful to build lead magnets and freebies that people sign up for, receive and then I can nurture them with an email sequence. Newsletters have a higher conversion rate than social media followers. But the big zinger? You own the emails on your list. If you get locked out of your account on Facebook or get hacked. You lose those followers for good and have to start over. Email lists stay and build. Even if you don't have a lot of content, I 100% believe your time will be better off spent posting a couple times a week on social media, but being proactive growing your email list.

In summary, building an online presence and using social media can be overwhelming, but it doesn't have to be boring. Choose the right platform, be human, engage with your followers, create engaging content, and don't neglect the basics to really make your social media presence crescendo to new heights!

Finding Where Your Ideal Client Is

It's important to reach your ideal clients where they hang out online. But how do you know where that is? Here are some comical tips to help you find the perfect platform:

Ask your mom friends- because let's face it, moms know everything. They have Facebook groups that are for moms. They know the best meet opportunities and can help spread the word in the community. Give your favorite mom friend a few of your business cards and ask her to go wild. At the very least she probably has a friend who's a Facebook addict and another who's obsessed with Instagram. Get those around you a mega phone and let them go wild.

Go on a social media safari- put on your khaki shorts and safari hat and venture out into the wilds of social media. Observe your target audience in their natural habitat and take note of where they congregate.

Conduct a poll- create a poll on social media asking your followers which platforms they use most often. Don't forget to include a silly response option like "I still use MySpace".

Make a lead Magnet- Sometimes it's as simple as makinga few free music worksheets and using your newsletter site to host your lead magnet and deliver it. Example "Free music workbook" Fill out your name and email and where you saw this. Bam, now you know where the audience that YOU want is hanging out.

In all seriousness, finding the platform your ideal client is on takes some research and trial and error. But with a little humor and creativity, you'll be sure to find the perfect platform to take your studio's online presence to new heights.

Building a positive reputation through customer service and community involvement

Let's talk about how to build a positive reputation for your music studio through customer service, community involvement, and volunteer opportunities.

First things first, let's talk about customer service. As a music studio owner, it's important to provide your clients with a top-notch experience. You want them to leave each lesson feeling satisfied and excited to come back for more. One way to do this is by offering excellent customer service. This means being friendly, approachable, and responsive to your clients' needs. If they have a question or concern, address it promptly and with a positive attitude. And if they give you feedback, take it constructively and use it to improve your services.

Now let's move on to community involvement. As a small business owner, it's important to be an active member of your community. This means attending local events, sponsoring local charities, and getting involved in community initiatives. Not only does this show that you care about your community, but it also helps to spread the word about your business. People are more likely to support a business that is actively involved in its community.

Lastly, let's talk about volunteer opportunities. Volunteering is a great way to give back to your community while also building your reputation as a business owner. You can volunteer at local schools, community centers, or even at local music events. By volunteering, you're not only helping others, but you're also showing your commitment to your community and your passion for music.

Building a positive reputation for your music studio takes a combination of excellent customer service, community involvement, and volunteer opportunities. By doing these things, you'll be well on your way to building a successful and respected music studio. Keep on rockin'!

Chapter 15: Harmony
Balancing Work and Life

Finding a balance between work and family life

Ah, the elusive balance! Finding harmony between work and family life is like trying to play a perfect chord on a guitar. It takes practice, patience, and a lot of fine-tuning. But fear not, my fellow musicians, I'm here to share some tips on how to make it work. I know I talk about this in another section but here I am giving you permission to say no to work, and yes to your life. Life imitates art. Don't push your business so much that you burn the line between work and your creative passion.

First things first, set boundaries. Just like you wouldn't let a bandmate walk all over you during a rehearsal, you shouldn't let work consume your entire life. Create a schedule and stick to it. When it's time to work, focus on work. When it's time to be with family, focus on family.

Second, prioritize what's important. Is it really necessary to check your work email at 11 PM when you could be spending quality time with your loved ones. Probably not. Determine what truly matters and make it a priority.

Third, learn to say no. It's okay to turn down a gig or project if it conflicts with your personal life. Don't be afraid to put your foot down and say, "Sorry, I can't do that right now."

Fourth, delegate tasks. Just like you would delegate parts to different band members, delegate household chores and responsibilities to your family members. You don't have to do it all yourself.

Finally, don't forget to take care of yourself. Just like you wouldn't neglect your instrument, don't neglect your own well-being. Take breaks, exercise, and do things that bring you joy and fulfillment outside of work and family.

Remember, finding harmony between work and family life is a process. It won't happen overnight, but with some practice and patience, you can create a beautiful melody that brings balance to your life.

Managing stress and burnout

Hey there, rockstar. It's time to hit pause and take a breath. Owning a music studio is no easy gig, and the long hours and high demands can quickly lead to burnout. But fear not, my friend. With a little bit of rhythm and some solid self-care strategies, you can find your work-life groove and keep on jamming.

My story: I have wanted both a Youtube channel and a Podcast for about ten years. This year I finally launched both and was so excited. But, in all my excitement I quickly burned out. On top of the time it took to record, edit, and publish, I had a deadline always on my mind. Why? What is the urgency? Finally, I realized for my mental health, it was best to not have a deadline. If that means not posting every week. Thats fine. It's not my main source of income. I don't have to worry about losing money by making listeners wait. It will be there when I have the time. We all have those side projects and even projects that could benefit the business. Always run it through a filter, is this going to add value to my day-to-day life, or disrupt it? You have no deadline to extra list items except for the ones you set yourself.

Let's talk about stress. It's no secret that running a business can be stressful. Even though stress can occasionally be helpful in small doses by motivating you to push through challenges and reach new heights. It's also a detriment to health. When the body is stressed it likes to fight harder in the wrong ways and suddenly our immune system is under attack. We are business owners in the service industry. If we are sick, we don't teach. If we don't teach, we don't make money. The key is to manage stress in a healthy way so that it doesn't become overwhelming. This of course is different for everyone but I will give a few examples.

How do we do that:

One of the best ways to manage stress is to stay organized and prioritize your tasks. Make a to-do list and tackle the most important items first. And don't forget to take breaks throughout the day. A quick walk around the block or a five-minute meditation can work wonders for your mental health.

Another helpful strategy for managing stress is to delegate tasks whenever possible. You don't have to do everything yourself, and hiring help can actually save you time and energy in the long run. Plus, it's a great opportunity to support other musicians and create a community of like-minded individuals.

Speaking of community, don't forget to take time for yourself and your loved ones. It's easy to get caught up in work and forget about the other important things in life, but balance is key. Schedule in time for family, friends, and hobbies that bring you joy. Remember, you're not just a music studio owner, you're a multi-dimensional human being with a life outside of work.

Finally, if you find yourself feeling burnt out, take a break. It's okay to step back and recharge your batteries. Whether it's a weekend getaway, a staycation, or simply a day off to binge-watch your favorite show, give yourself permission to rest and relax. Your mental health will thank you.

So there you have it, my friend. A few tips for finding your work-life groove and managing stress and burnout. Keep on jamming, and remember to take care of yourself along the way.

Practicing self-care and prioritizing your well-being

As a busy parent running a music studio, it's easy to put yourself last on the list of priorities. But let me tell you, taking care of yourself is like tuning your instrument before a big performance – it's essential for optimal performance!

So, let's talk about self-care. No, not just taking a bubble bath with a glass of wine (although that is always nice!). I'm talking about doing things that truly recharge your batteries and give you the energy you need to keep juggling all those responsibilities.

Maybe it's going for a run or doing some yoga. Maybe it's reading a book or listening to a podcast. Or maybe it's just taking a nap – no shame in that game!

But self-care is more than just fitting in some "me time" here and there. It's also about making your health and well-being a priority in your daily routine. That means eating well, staying hydrated, and getting enough sleep. It also means setting boundaries and saying "no" when you need to.

Trust me, your family, your students, and your business will all benefit when you're feeling your best. So go ahead, put on some soothing music, pour yourself a cup of tea, and take some time to care for yourself. You deserve it!

Chapter 16: Encore - Growing Your Business

Evaluating your progress and growth

Welcome to Chapter 16, the Encore! In this chapter, we will discuss the important topic of evaluating your progress and growth. But before we get into the nitty-gritty details, let me ask you a question: have you ever looked back at old photos of yourself and cringed at your questionable fashion choices? I know I have!

Well, evaluating your progress and growth is kind of like that. It's taking a step back, looking at where you started and seeing how far you've come. It's a chance to celebrate your successes and learn from your mistakes.

First things first, let's talk about metrics. These are the fancy numbers and data that show how well your business is doing. But let's be real, who actually understands all that jargon? Don't worry, you don't have to be a math wizard to evaluate your progress. Just look at your bank account! If there's money in there, you're doing something right.

Next, think about your goals. Have you achieved them? Are they still relevant? Maybe you set a goal to teach 50 students in a year, but now you realize that's too many to handle. It's okay to adjust your goals as you go along. In fact, it's encouraged! Just make sure they're still challenging and inspiring.

Finally, don't forget to celebrate your successes! Throw yourself a party, treat yourself to a fancy latte, or binge-watch your favorite show. You deserve it! And remember, growth takes time. Be patient with yourself and your business.

Expanding your services and offerings

You've made it to the encore, where you get to show off all the hard work you've put into your music studio. But just because you've reached this point doesn't mean it's time to stop growing. In fact, it's time to start expanding your services and offerings. Think about it - your students come to you to learn music, but what else could you offer them? Here are some ideas to get your creative juices flowing:

Music camps: Why not host a music camp during the summer or over school breaks? This gives your students a chance to really dive into music and have a fun experience outside of regular lessons.

Recording sessions: If you have the space and equipment, why not offer recording sessions to your students? This is a great way to give them a taste of what it's like to record in a studio.

Music therapy: If you have a background in music therapy, consider offering this service to your students. Music can be a powerful tool for emotional and physical healing.

Group lessons: While one-on-one lessons are great, group lessons can also be beneficial. They allow for collaboration and socialization among students. This has been the best expansion I have done in my personal studio. I created my own system and now I am known for group opportunities in our area. Do some research and see if there is a need. It's a wonderful way to increase your hourly wage times four or five, while only adding on an extra hour per class, instead of the hour of weekly prep you do per student.

Instrument rental: If your students are just starting out, they may not have their own instrument yet. Consider offering instrument rental services to make it easier for them to get started.

Technician: If you know how to tune a piano. Then please move to my area in Alaska. We need you. Well, let's just say there is a high demand for quality piano techs. If you are able to learn, or already able to work on acoustics, this is a great way to make an additional income.

Subbing: It's always worth looking into the opportunity to be a substitute teacher in your school district. Not only does this build authority and trust in your community, but if you are a music substitute then you are in the room with potential students. Of course your not going to be handing out your business card or offering your service, but those kids know you as a musician. When they want lessons, they will recognize you as someone they know. That is valuable.

Expanding your services not only benefits your students, but it can also help your business grow. Just remember to stay true to your values and keep the focus on providing quality music education.

Planning for long-term success and fulfillment

Let's talk about how to plan for long-term success and fulfillment. And don't worry, I won't bore you with all those fancy business terms. I'll keep it fun and simple, just like playing a catchy tune.

Step 1: Dream big, but be realistic. It's important to have a clear vision of where you want your business to go. Do you want to expand your services or open a new location? Or maybe you want to focus on improving your current services and customer experience. Whatever your dream is, make sure it's achievable and aligns with your values and goals. Refer back to the business plan you were supposed to make.

Step 2: Create a roadmap. A roadmap is like a music sheet, it helps you stay on track and reach your goals. Break down your long-term vision into smaller achievable goals with timelines. This will help you stay accountable and track your progress.

Step 3: Keep learning and evolving. The music industry is constantly changing and evolving. It's important to stay up to date with the latest trends and techniques in your field. Attend conferences, workshops, and networking events. Collaborate with other professionals and stay curious.

Step 4: Take care of yourself. Your business is only as good as you are. Take breaks, practice self-care, and prioritize your well-being. Remember, you're not a robot, you're a human being.

Step 5: Celebrate your successes. Don't forget to take a moment to celebrate your achievements. You've worked hard and deserve to feel proud of your accomplishments. Celebrate with your team, family, and friends.

In conclusion, planning for long-term success and fulfillment is like composing a symphony. It takes time, practice, and dedication. But with the right mindset and approach, you can create a beautiful masterpiece that will last a lifetime.

Recap

Well, you've made it this far and have established a successful music studio. But the journey doesn't stop here. It's time to take your business to the next level and start thinking about growth. Here are some tips to help you grow your business:

Expand your services: Consider offering new services, such as music production or music therapy, to attract a wider audience and increase revenue. I started offering online courses and it has been wildly successful.

Network and collaborate: Attend music conferences and events, join local business groups, and collaborate with other music professionals to expand your reach and build new relationships.

Invest in marketing: Develop a strong marketing plan to reach potential clients and build brand awareness. Consider using social media ads, email marketing campaigns, and targeted promotions to reach your ideal audience.

Hire staff: If you're feeling overwhelmed, consider hiring additional staff to help with administrative tasks, teaching, and managing the studio.

Seek funding: If you're looking to expand your studio, consider seeking funding from investors or applying for a small business loan to help finance your growth.

Remember, growing your business takes time and effort, but with the right strategies in place, you can take your music studio to new heights.

Achieving Your Dream Job as a Private Music Studio Owner

You made it to the end of this guide on building your dream job as a private music studio owner. By now, you should have gained valuable insights on the various aspects of starting and growing your own music studio, from setting up your business plan to creating a curriculum and lesson plans, hiring and managing instructors, collaborating with other professionals, and achieving long-term success and fulfillment.

Remember that building a successful music studio takes time, effort, and dedication. But with the right mindset, tools, and strategies, you can achieve your dream job as a private music studio owner and make a positive impact on the lives of your students and community.

As you move forward, keep these key takeaways in mind:

Passion and purpose are the driving forces behind any successful business.

Effective planning and organization are essential for setting and achieving your goals.

Continuous learning, innovation, and adaptation are crucial for staying competitive and relevant in the ever-changing world of music education.

Building a supportive and collaborative network of professionals and organizations can help you expand your reach and impact.

Prioritizing self-care, work-life balance, and fulfillment is key to sustaining your passion and success over the long term.

Write the next steps you need to take in order to create your business.

☐

☐

☐

☐

☐

Thank you for joining me on this journey. I wish you all the best in building your dream job as a private music studio owner, and may your music continue to inspire and transform the world! Keep an eye out for all my new offerings at https://greenhousemusicak.com . New books, videos, trainings, and tips are on the way.

Delana

www.ingramcontent.com/pod-product-compliance
Lightning Source LLC
Chambersburg PA
CBHW070318240526
45467CB00046B/1890